Alice

or

A Most Happy Childhood

Elizabeth Laughton Corney

DEDICATION

Dedicated to my mother Alice, née Goodacre, (born 1894, died 1982). She made this book possible by recounting all these true childhood memories and escapades, giving an insight into a Victorian farming family's life.

CONTENTS

ACKNOWLEDGMENTS

With grateful thanks to Lydie, Gina, Stephen and Richard for their invaluable help.

1 SPRING DAYS

It was Lady day in March when farm workers went to the market place and stood waiting to be hired for another year by one of the many farmers of the fen country. Alice and her brothers and sisters hurried home from the village school. The March wind bowled them along, dust flurries blowing around their chubby little legs as they ran down the country lanes. The flat fen country provided meagre shelter from the wind and rain; only the hedges and low wooded hills breaking the weather moving in from the east. Birch and alder catkins shed their yellow pollen in golden clouds as the wind shook them and whistled through the dry branches of the gnarled and twisted shrub oaks. Pollarded willows and hawthorn hedges showed a faint tinge of spring green matched by the growing wheat in the fields. In the copses bluebell spears pushed through the carpet of last years' leaves and the birds were busy foraging in these for sleepy insects not yet brought to life by the pale spring sun.

The children's footsteps rang hollowly on the plank bridges over the drainage dykes which criss-crossed the countryside like silver silken threads. With heads bent before the wind the little family could not get home quickly enough. Would Father be back yet from the market? Had he been hired as a farm labourer or horseman for another year? Another move might be in the offing; if so a lot of work lay ahead. The children burst into the farm cottage all speaking at once.

"Are we moving Father?"

"Where are we going?"

"Can we take our pets with us?"

Mother straightened up from where she had been stirring a delicious-smelling stew on the hob. She smiled to see their eager expectant faces. Alice the eldest, with clear brown eyes and unruly curls framing a strong characterful face; Nell, close in age and very aware of her pretty femininity; fair-haired Jim, a quiet boy; George, sturdily independent, and Jennie, small and dainty. Father was sitting in his high backed wooden armchair by the fire, sucking at the stem of his unlit pipe. The children held their breath and waited for him to speak.

"Yes, children," he said, "we move on Monday to Willowgarth. I am going to work for Mr. Hughes."

There was a sigh of escaping breath and the children all began talking again, asking questions and then hurrying on without waiting for any answers.

"How many bedrooms Father?"

"Is there a water tap inside the house?"

"Are there a lot of fruit trees in the garden?"

"Is there an attic?"

"That's enough," said Father quietly and there was immediate silence. Father spoke seldom but when he did he was instantly obeyed. "Jim, George, we still have our jobs to do here. Alice, Nell and Jennie help Mother with the tea", and Father went to change into his working clothes.

Moving day dawned fine and clear. The children had been busy all weekend helping Mother pack the best china, the kitchen utensils and their clothes and toys. The farm buildings had been searched for any of Father's tools, curtains and bedding had been washed, and carpets rolled up after a good beating on the washing line.

Chattering like magpies the children helped carry the furniture out and load it onto the farm cart. The girls had to wait impatiently whilst Father, with George and Jim, drove the cart the few miles to their new home, unloaded and returned for the final journey. Mother kept the girls busy sweeping out the empty rooms of the old house ready for the next family to move into. Never let it be said that Mother left a dirty house behind. Then it was onto the cart for the ride to their new home, the girls clinging tightly to the rope-tied bundles of bedding as the cart trundled over the ruts in the lane.

Willowgarth was a farm cottage at the end of a long lane, some miles away, near another village. As Father drew the cart to a halt the girls clambered down and raced into the empty dwelling. George and Jim, who had been left in charge during Father's second trip, very importantly showed their sisters round their new home. Downstairs

Willowgarth Cottage

was a large living kitchen and a parlour. As the girls stood on the threshold looking at soon to be familiar surroundings, George pulled them into the kitchen.

"Look," he said. There, just above the stone sink in the corner was a water tap. The children danced and shouted with glee around the stone-flagged room. No more fetching water for Mother from the outside pump. Better still, no more washing outside on a freezing winter morning, vainly trying to coax a trickle of water through the icicles hanging from the pump. Laughing with delight at such luxury they raced through the rest of the house. A large pantry, back kitchen and wash house led out of the living kitchen, and in one corner a curving staircase led up to three bedrooms on the first floor.

Above these and reached by narrow rickety stairs, were two tiny attics. After a quick inspection the children hurried out to help unload the cart. Father and George had the first important task – to sweep the chimney.

George loved helping Father do this. Climbing like a monkey onto the cottage roof, he lowered a rope weighted with a brick down the wide chimney pot. When it reached the fireplace Father tied a holly bush onto the rope and then he and George pulled it slowly up the chimney. This dislodged any soot which fell into the dust sheets Mother had fastened over the hearth in the cottage. The girls cheered and encouraged their brother to show off as he capered across the roof to the parlour chimney, teeth gleaming whitely in his soot-grimed face.

This job done and the soot removed, a fire was the next thing, to heat pans of water for scrubbing floors and washing paint. With the windows flung wide to let in the fresh country air, the curtains were hung, furniture placed in position and the beds made. After a huge tea of bread and dripping followed by home-made fruit cake, Mother carried in the tin bath and the children had a warm wash in front of the kitchen fire before falling into bed more tired than they ever remembered .

Next morning the hens had to be housed and clean straw found for their nesting boxes; the cow shed and stables cleaned out; a sheltered place found for the rabbit hutch and a secure box found for George's ferret.

"We don't want that smelly thing near our rabbits," said fastidious Jennie. George took the ferret from his jacket pocket where it spent most of its time He stroked the sharp-nosed, creamily smooth little animal, letting it get perilously near to Jennie who edged back in alarm.

"Alright George," said Mother, "there are plenty of chores for all of you to do for me, but you can take your pet and make a secure cage for it in the back of the stable."

Mother managed to whitewash all the inside walls of the cottage in the first three days of occupancy, but at last she said the children could leave her to finish settling in, and they were free! Free to run down strange country lanes and wonder what new delights would unfold round the next corner. The girls were free to find secret paths and hidden places in the wood, and pussy willow and early primroses in the hedges. The boys were free to see where the birds were building their nests, find frog spawn and minnows in the stream at the end of the lane. Father had already started working for his new employer and was busy planting the spring corn, guiding one of his teams of powerful shire horses as it pulled the seed drill up and down the furrows.

Resting from their explorations the girls sat on the top of one of the five-barred gates and watched. "Father's faithful friends" Alice called the horses; the jingling of the shining brasses on their spotless harness and the rhythmic plodding of their hooves making sweet music in the spring sunshine. The working harness on many farm horses was often dull, unpolished and tied together with odd pieces of leather or string. Father loved his horses and believed they should have the best of everything as a reward for the hard work they did for the farmer.

"Back to school in the morning," said Mother at teatime one day when they were all sitting round the large wooden table in the kitchen. The younger children groaned but Alice smiled. The journey to their new school meant a walk of nearly three miles, but everyone was used to walking in the stout laced leather boots they wore. If it was cold in the mornings Mother would give them all a hot baked potato to hold, which kept their hands warm and provided a snack when they got to school. The teacher would put their dinner containers round the huge iron stove in the schoolroom, and the carefully packed pies or stew stayed warm till mid-day. Alice enjoyed school. There was always something interesting to do.

"Now Alice," said Mother in the morning, "here is a letter for the teacher with all your birth dates and details of which other schools you have been to. Take care of the little ones and don't dawdle on the way home."

It was a pleasant walk along the lanes, and the children passed several interesting-looking places which they hoped to explore in the holidays. When they reached the village they had only to follow the sounds of laughing, shouting voices to find the school. As they entered the playground they felt themselves the centre of interest and were glad to go into the building to meet the schoolmaster. After reading the explanatory note from their mother he showed the children where to hang their coats and put their lunch baskets.

The school building was of red brick, with one big high pointed ceilinged room criss-crossed by dark oaken rafters. The large pointed windows were set high in the walls so the children could not waste time looking out, although the glimpses of sunny skies and scudding clouds caused many a sore knuckle – rapped with a ruler – when thoughts soared freely to join the high flying birds. Divided in half by a heavy curtain, the large schoolroom contained two classes: the older boys and girls working behind it at one end, and the babies at the other. The schoolmaster, who sometimes had an assistant, took all the lessons, and the schoolhouse where he lived joined onto the school building. In the cloakroom were rows of iron coat hooks and a large sink with a cold-water tap. The lavatories, across the yard, were just a long bench with two or three holes in, over open pits in the earth floor. Sited on a slight slope, the waste matter from the lavatories was shovelled out through trap doors and taken away in a soil cart by one of the farmers on contract to the school authorities.

The scholars were allowed to take it in turns to ring the brass hand bell, and the new pupils looked apprehensively at each other as the orderly lines of boys and girls marched into school. All hands were inspected for cleanliness and each child had to produce a clean handkerchief. Jennie and George, tightly holding hands, were taken to join the group of younger children and Alice, Nell and Jim sent to sit at the back of the main class. The iron-framed desks with their wooden bench seats and sloping wooden tops were well carved with initials. Before Alice left George with the younger children she noticed how he was rubbing his hand thoughtfully over the indentations, and gave him a warning kick on the ankle. He was only allowed to keep a penknife on the understanding that he used it properly.

Alice loved the orderliness of the school routine and the blissful silence when everyone was busy working. At home it was seldom quiet and there were seemingly endless jobs to be done. Lessons in reading, writing and arithmetic were interspersed with geography, history, scripture, singing, needlework and nature study. The babies would chant their letters and words, the older pupils their multiplication tables. Writing was practised on a slate with a slate pencil which set Alice's teeth on edge when it squeaked, although as you progressed through school you were allowed to use pen and ink. Most of the girls made themselves a little flannel booklet in the needlework lessons with which to wipe their pen nibs and so avoid making blots on their books.

The children soon settled down in their new school. They were used to moving from place to place as Father was hired every year to work in different areas. School life in the small village communities revolved round the farming year. Nearly all the menfolk were connected with the land either as farmers, labourers, herdsmen, horsemen, shepherds and dairymen or indirectly as blacksmiths, farriers, wheelwrights, carpenters, dry-stone wallers and hedge layerers. The seasons were important, and country customs observed. It was taken for granted that the older boys would help on the farm at harvest time and the older girls would stay at home during a mother's confinement. There was a regular week's holiday in October for potato picking. Most of the boys would follow their father's occupation when they left school, though some would join the Army or Navy. The girls would go into service as parlour maids, cooks or nursemaids. For one or two outstanding pupils there was a chance of going to the Grammar school or High school if they passed a scholarship.

On Empire Day, when everyone marched smartly into the school yard and proudly sang "God Save The Queen" whilst the Union Jack fluttered from the flagpole, Alice used to think of all the people living in distant lands under the protection of the Queen's soldiers and sailors. Did not the gypsies who came to the markets and horse fairs come from a far-off land? They certainly had brown skins – rather like the stains on her hands when she had been picking walnuts for Mother. George and Jim stood stiffly to attention, little hands clenched by their sides, hearts bursting with pride. They were going to join the Queen's Navy when they were old enough.

The spring days lengthened and the signs of new life were all around: primroses and cowslips on the grassy banks, pink campion and ragged robin in the hedgerows.

"Don't bring any of that into the house," warned George solemnly as Nell gathered a shimmering bouquet of white lacy cow parsley, "it's called mother die and Mother will die." Nell dashed the flowers to the ground and burst into tears.

Frog spawn and tadpoles populated the drainage ditches. The birds sang their love songs, built their nests, and the sun rose higher in the sky every day. Mother planted vegetables, flower and herb seeds in the cottage garden, and sent the boys with Father to cut straight willow twigs from the trees which grew on the banks of the stream. She carefully peeled the bark from these twigs and wove them into baskets. The girls were then despatched to the rough pasture and field margins to fill the baskets with succulent young nettles which she boiled as a vegetable or brewed into nettle beer. This was a most refreshing drink, and the children were quite used to drinking various home-made beers as the water was not safe to drink unless it was first boiled. The girls were glad of the long woollen stockings they wore which protected their legs from the stinging hairs on the nettles. Hands and arms were often nettled but soon became cool and soothed by the application of juice from bruised dock leaves which always seemed to grow near a nettle bed.

George came running home one day from cutting willows with a deep gash in his thumb. He had pressed his fingers over the wound but it was bleeding quite badly. The girls gasped when they saw him but Mother calmly said:

"Quickly Alice fetch me some bandage." As Alice darted into the kitchen to get some strips of old but clean sheeting stored for this very purpose in the big chest of drawers, Mother went out into the stable returning almost immediately with a large wispy cobweb in her hand. With the girls watching in amazement, she rinsed George's thumb then placed the cobweb over the cut, drawing the edges of the wound together as she did so. Firmly bandaging the cobweb into place she then lectured George on the correct way to use a sharp knife.

"Why did you use a cobweb Mother?" the girls wanted to know after George had thankfully departed.

"An old Irishman once used one on your father's leg, "and I have never forgotten how well it healed." Certainly George's thumb seemed to heal very quickly.

In the rough pasture near the cottage were several fruit trees: apple, plum and a tall pear tree. A pair of blackbirds decided that the upper branches of the pear tree were safely out of reach of the farm cats and any other threat to their fledglings, and built their nest well above the ground. George loved climbing and collecting birds' eggs. The high nest in the tall tree was a challenge, and one day he set off like a monkey, scrambling up the stout trunk. His heavy, thick-soled boots provided a good purchase on the rough bark and he was soon in the lower branches. Nell and Jennie, who had been playing with their doll and carriage nearby, stood transfixed as they saw him climb still higher, balancing precariously to reach into the nest and remove a speckled blue egg. The parent birds flew about the tree calling in great distress but even this did not stop him.

Alice joined her sisters and the three girls, hardly daring to breathe, watched their brother as he triumphantly placed the egg in his trouser pocket and began to climb down. Careless in his success, he missed his footing and, amidst the terrible noise of breaking branches, fell through the lower part of the tree to crash to the ground in a shower of leaves and twigs. Whilst Jennie gathered up her skirts and raced to fetch Mother, Alice and Nell ran to the quiet form lying still and pale on the ground. Nell burst into tears but George groaned, opened his eyes and, with brotherly scorn, told her to stop blubbing. By the time Mother arrived he was getting to his feet, pale and bruised but otherwise sound in wind and limb. The only sign of his misdemeanour was a damp yellow patch on his trousers where the fragile egg had been messily destroyed.

Undeterred by this episode he was bird nesting again a few days later. Father had shown him where a partridge had made its nest in a hollow between two furrows in the wheat field. There, hidden by the growing wheat was a clutch of earth-brown eggs. Coming home from school he lagged behind the others, and when they had turned a corner in the lane and were out of sight, he pushed his way as quietly as possible through the hedge and into the field. Making sure he was unobserved he quickly transferred the eggs from the nest to his cap and then hurried home to show his prize to Mother. Mother was extremely angry.

"You can just go and put them back," she ordered. George scowled darkly.

"Someone might see me."

"Serve you right then," said Mother. "I only hope it isn't the constable."

Poor George. It was a crime to take the eggs of game birds.

Reluctantly he skulked slowly back to the field. Full of self-righteousness the three sisters followed at a distance, although they were ready to warn him if danger approached. To everyone's relief they were able to report his success in replacing the eggs, and as spring blossomed into summer the children were pleased to see partridge chicks near the site of the nest.

2 THE VIOLIN

Alice stayed behind after school one day, helping to tidy away the slates and pencils, and it was then that she first heard the older pupils having their violin lesson. She watched entranced as Mr. Baker, the visiting music master, picked up a shiny brown instrument which had long strings stretched down one side of it. He held a stick in his right hand and, tucking one end of the brown box under his chin, drew the stick across the strings on the box. Alice heard tuneful, melodic sounds coming from the box and she crouched down, partly hidden by the curtain dividing the two classrooms, as several of the girls played their instruments. Did the girls realise how fortunate they were being able to hold such a lovely musical instrument and coax tunes from it? Apart from Mother's cheerful singing about the house, all the music Alice had heard had been played either on Father's concertina, the school piano or the chapel organ. Now here was this strange box of wood that she longed to touch and see if she could play a tune. A "violin" she had heard Mr. Baker call it.

With a start she realised how late it was. If the little ones arrived home without her, there would be trouble. Taking off her elastic garters and rolling down her long black woollen stockings, she raced out of the school playground and ran like the wind to catch up with her younger brothers and sisters as they turned down the farm lane.

"Our Alice didn't catch us up till the top of the lane," said Nell virtuously, as they went into the kitchen of the cottage.

"Tell-tale tit, your tongue will split," taunted George.

"She wants a violin," piped up Jennie.

Mother said nothing but turned and smiled at her eldest daughter.

"Oh Mother," burst out Alice. "I would love to have violin lessons. Please, please can I learn to play?"

"I don't know," replied Mother. "Find out about it and we'll see what we can do."

Alice did her chores in a dream, and next day asked at school about the cost of hiring a violin and having some lessons. When she reported home, Mother sadly shook her head.

"I'm sorry Alice but we just can't manage to pay for the violin and the lessons."

"I'll pay for my lessons," pleaded Alice "if you could manage to get the violin."

"I'll talk it over with Father," promised Mother.

How could she get the money to pay for lessons wondered Alice. There was only the occasional copper to spare and she would need nine pence a week for her lessons from Mr. Baker. Deep in thought, she walked slowly home from school that day. As she passed the inn which marked the halfway point between the farm and the village, old Mrs. Swaine, the landlady, came out and spoke to her.

"Now then Alice, you're looking very serious about something."

The young girl poured out the story and how she was willing to do anything to pay for music lessons. Under her white mob cap the old lady's eyes twinkled and she smiled down at the earnest little girl standing before her.

"Well," said Mrs. Swaine, "it so happens that I need someone to wash the beer and wine glasses in the back kitchen. If your ma says you can do them for me – and you must come every day after school, I will pay you nine pence a week."

"Oh thank you Mrs. Swaine," she gasped before racing home to tell her parents.

So it was arranged. Every evening, and Saturday after lunch, Alice went into the back kitchen of the inn and washed the used glasses. Mrs. Swaine was very particular. Her little helper was swathed in a spotless white linen apron before she went to the two large wooden bowls standing in the stone sink. One was filled with hot soapy water, and in this Alice had to thoroughly wash the dirty glasses. The evening sun streaming through the small-paned kitchen window highlighted the lovely rainbow colours of the soapy bubbles in the glasses, and sometimes Alice would fill one with the sparkling lather and pretend it was beer. The washed glasses were then transferred to the second bowl which contained hot water tinted with dolly blue – a washing aid which was also good for soothing bee stings. After a thorough rinsing, the glasses were turned upside down and left on a lead sink to drain.

Mother saw how determined her daughter was and arranged to hire the violin, paying the charge weekly from the money she obtained selling butter at the market. What joy when Alice had her first lesson, learning to hold the bow just so and play on the open strings. She rushed home to show the family. Mother wrinkled her nose when Alice took the violin from its case.

"It smells like a coffin," she remarked. The girl thought coffins must smell very nice if they smelt like her violin.

As Alice drew her bow across the strings, George made a face and put his fingers in his ears.

"Sounds like a rabbit after my Ferdie's had it," he said. Ferdie was his pet ferret who was often seen poking his head out of George's jacket pocket.

"You'll have to practise in the attic," said Mother. "I can't do with that noise down here."

Undaunted, Alice went up to the cold attic and there, night after night by candlelight and sometimes in the early mornings, she worked away at her music. Her hands were often so blue and numb that she could hardly hold the violin, and her finger ends were sore from pressing on the strings. After playing she would wrap the instrument reverently in a soft yellow duster, loosen the horse hair bow and place it and the violin in its wooden case. Mother could sometimes hear her playing and was really rather proud of her eldest daughter.

One morning old Mr. Anderson came to the farm to clean out the dykes. Dressed in his moleskin coat and breeches tied at the knees with string, he was a familiar figure in the countryside as he walked along the lanes, the tools of his trade resting on his shoulder. The eels he caught in the drainage ditches made a welcome change from the usual farm diet. Mother would skin and chop the eels, then simmer them slowly with lots of vegetables in the fireside oven. They were delicious. Mr. Anderson was also a very good violinist, much in demand to play at weddings and dances, and he heard Alice practising one day.

"I'm sure she's good enough for the orchestra" said Mother as Alice played "The Bluebells of Scotland" and two variations.

"Not yet," replied Mr. Anderson "but she's doing alright. Why not enter her for the Music Festival."

With the help of Mr. Baker Alice learnt the pieces for the Festival. Even Jim and George had to admit that they could recognise the tunes. On the appointed day everyone got up especially early. Mother and Alice were to catch the carrier's cart at the end of the lane for a ride to town where the Festival was being held. Nell and Jennie felt very important as they had to make sure their brothers got safely to school – much to George's disgust.

"We're not babbies you know," he told Mother indignantly.

As Alice got dressed in her best navy blue dress with a pointed white lace collar, best black stockings and highly polished black buttoned boots, her sisters came and hugged her warmly.

"Here's my best white ribbon for your hair," said Nell.

"Play your bestest Ally," said Jennie "and you can have my lace hanky for your pocket."

"Thank you dears," and Alice picked up her violin and ran downstairs to where Mother was waiting. The ride in the carrier's cart seemed endless. Usually, if she went with Mother to market, Alice enjoyed the chatter as the housewives exchanged news and gossip. Sitting on the bench seat, warm comfy bodies pressed close on either side, baskets filled with home-made goodies balanced on plump knees, in the soft green glow of the tarpaulin cover she felt safe and secure. Today each bump and sway of the cart brought a very strange feeling to the pit of her stomach, and the incessant voices seemed muted and far away. The passing countryside was a blur of colour, and Alice was extremely relieved when the jolting of the cart announced their arrival in the cobbled market square. When she climbed down from the cart and saw all the other children converging on the Town Hall, her hands suddenly felt very clammy and she was glad of Jennie's handkerchief on which to wipe them.

The children were ushered into a cold, dark-panelled waiting room where their violins were tuned and each child handed a competitor number. They were instructed to remain silent during the playing, go onto the stage when their number was called, and sit in the auditorium after they had completed their entry.

Alice felt as overawed as everyone else looked, but after listening to several older children, her spirits began to lighten. Although she still had an inward trembling when she stepped onto the stage, once she began to play she forgot everything but her music.

To her delight she was awarded a First Class certificate, the adjudicator appearing pleased with her performance. Mother was happy too, and when all the family were sitting round the table at supper time, she and Alice had to recount in detail what had happened.

Father did not say much, but Alice realised how pleased he must have been when, a few days later, a letter and a parcel arrived for her. Alice had no idea what was in the strange-shaped parcel and examined it curiously.

"Oh do open it," begged her brothers and sisters. "Let's see what it is." Indeed a parcel by post was a rarity for the farming family.

"Can I cut the string for you with my penknife?" offered George impatiently as Alice carefully untied the knotted string and unfolded the thick brown paper. The lid of the wooden box inside was raised to reveal a scratched and battered but beautifully toned violin. The children all gasped with delight and pleasure.

"Read the letter," commanded Father gruffly.

The letter was from an aunt of Father's saying how delighted she was to hear from him of Alice's interest in music, and how hard she must have worked to reach such a good standard The violin was a gift which great-aunt hoped would be useful and give Alice a lot of happiness. The little girl's face pinkened with pleasure, and after she had lovingly polished the instrument with a soft duster, she sat down and painstakingly wrote a very grateful "thank you" letter.

3 A COUNTRY FAMILY

Father was head of the little household. He was tall, grave-faced with deep-set blue eyes, one of which was blind after being kicked in the face by a spring lamb. He had a ginger moustache, weather-beaten complexion and work worn hands. As she grew older, Alice realised that behind his gruff voice and rough exterior was a deep thinking proud man, who genuinely loved his family. Working from dawn to dusk as he did, much of the everyday disciplining of the young ones was left to Mother, but sometimes he had to put a word in. And one word was enough. The children had heard from other boys about fathers who used their leather belts on erring sons and, whilst Father's manner had never suggested he would resort to such punishment, they were not going to give him an excuse to try. When asked how he knew of their little misdemeanours – for he always seemed to know – he would say quietly "A little bird told me."

"When I catch that bird I'll wring its dratted neck," muttered George darkly.

When Father came in from the fields, Mother always had a cup of tea ready for him. Too hot to drink straight from the cup, he would pour some of the tea into the saucer, blow on it to cool it, then noisily sip it through his moustache. The boys used to watch him enviously but dare not copy his example – not since George had earned a clip on the ear for trying.

Father was an extremely taciturn man who did not suffer fools gladly. He had infinite patience with the animals on the farm, but only showed the boys or men under him twice how to do a job. After that they had to learn by experience. It was a joy to watch him with his horses. He trained them to pull the plough, harrow or rake, with the minimum of fuss, obviously feeling an affinity with the big shires. The children would walk up and down the furrows listening as he gave his gentle but firm commands. "Hup" meant start, "whoa" stop. Pulling on the right rein guided the pair of plough horses to the right and on the left one to the left. When training a new horse, Father would yoke it to an older experienced one, and so ease the task of teaching. When the reins went slack the horse knew to stop, and when Father gathered the reins, the horses tensed their strong muscles to start work again.

All the children helped to clean the harness, rubbing the reins, hames and collars with saddle soap prior to buffing with a soft cloth. The horse brasses shone after polishing, and Father insisted on the buckles being polished as well. Some of the tack had little porcelain studs which were decorated with daintily painted flowers. When Father entered any of the stock in the village agricultural shows, he took great pains with their grooming. Sometimes he had a shire mare with foal at foot, and then the nimble fingers of the girls were required to plait and tie manes and braid the tails of the mother and baby.

Father looked a real "masher"

Father liked the horses in another way too. He spent his meagre money allowance at the racecourse. Alice thought he looked a real "masher" when he took a day off to go to the races. Entirely different from his everyday clothes (winceyette shirt, rough-tweed jacket, trousers tied round the knee with string, flat cap for

it was drastic treatment, but it worked, drawing out all the poisonous matter.

Similarly, linseed poultices were applied to badly bruised or sprained limbs. The remedy worked on horses so why not on people? Bumps on heads were treated with cold-water compresses and an exhortation to "watch where you're going in future."

"Worse things happen at sea" was one of Mother's favourite sayings, and the children soon learned not to make a fuss over minor accidents, as they received scant sympathy from their parents.

Mother could find a use for most of the herbs which grew in the hedge bottoms or cottage gardens. Parsley had many uses: chewing cleared the breath after eating onions and a pad soaked in newly infused parsley tea soothed many a pair of tired eyes. Sties on eyes were cured with a rub of Mother's gold wedding ring, whilst a piece of grit in the eye was easily floated out when castor oil was dropped in the eye which was then covered with a large clean handkerchief. A horse hair tied tightly round the base of a wart soon caused it to die.

Comfrey was used in many ways for its healing powers. Camomile tea was a popular remedy with Mother for upset tummies. The children disliked it, but hated even more the annual "blood cleansing" treatment of brimstone and treacle. There was no escaping the springtime dose, even nipping the nose to stop the taste was no good.

Nettle stings were rubbed with the juice of dock leaves, and a cooling solution of witch hazel was applied to minor bumps and bruises. Cloves were pressed onto aching teeth or tender gums and certainly brought some relief, though thankfully everyone seemed to have good strong teeth. This was due in no small measure to the excellent diet available, but Mother insisted it was also due to the fact that once a week the family brushed their teeth with a mixture of soot and salt instead of the usual daily care of salt alone.

Alice quite enjoyed the luxury of a cold, for then she was kept snug and warm, and a supper-time treat was a drink of warm milk flavoured with black treacle. Indigestion was cured with half a teaspoonful of bicarbonate of soda in hot water.

Many of the plants in the fields were eaten for food. Young dandelion leaves made a delicious sandwich; the roots being roasted and ground as a substitute for coffee. Nasturtium leaves were a spicy addition to a salad, and their seeds were pickled by Mother in the autumn.

Country folk helped each other at times of illness or accident. Mother often sent the girls on errands saying "take this beef tea to Mrs. Jones and bring back any washing", or "Look after the little ones Alice, whilst I go and help Mrs. Winter with her new baby."

It was soon realised when Father sent one of his men for a hurdle, that a serious accident had taken place, and then someone would ride as fast as possible on the farm bicycle for the doctor. Quite often an unconscious patient had come round by the time he arrived, and any minor surgery needed was performed on the spotless kitchen table. Most of the country doctors were appreciative of the medical lore passed down through generations of farming families, and it certainly made their task easier. The children absorbed much without realising it.

As usual in a family each child differed in looks, character and temperament. The eldest, Alice, was often the ringleader in many of the scrapes the children got into. She had a quick mind, quick temper and speedy feet which usually got her out of the way of trouble. If there was anything she really wanted to do, she would work hard until she achieved it. Strong willed, yet generous of nature, she tried hard to be a help to Mother.

Alice was completely fearless. She stood her ground and refused to be browbeaten by her contemporaries. A drunken old tramp accosted the children one day as they walked home from school. Fortunately Father was working in a field adjoining the lane, but Alice shielded her two little sisters, sent George and Jim running for help and told the vagrant in no uncertain terms how ashamed he should be. Father made his presence known, but as the tramp shuffled off, Father smiled inwardly. Alice had been like a lioness defending her cubs.

Nell was two years younger than Alice. She was quite vain and jealously wanted what

Nell

everyone else had. Alice thought she had every reason to be vain with her large brown eyes and luxuriously thick, dark-brown hair. Nell was most upset when her sister said her eyes were like cows' eyes, although to Alice, cows' eyes were beautiful – liquid, gentle and brown with lovely long curling lashes. One of Nell's ambitions was to wear spectacles as she thought they were very smart. She would pretend to be unable to see the blackboard at school and at home-time, with eyes tightly shut, wanted to be led all the way as if she was blind. George soon put an end to that phase. Leading her home one afternoon he took her through all the muddy puddles, and when she tripped and fell full length in a pile of cow dung, laughed heartily and left her to cry all the way home.

Jennie, her name a shortened version of Jane Elizabeth, was named after one of her grandmothers. Small and dainty, Father called her his little butterfly. She tried to copy everything her older sisters did, particularly Nell who was her special friend. When Father came in from the fields at supper-time, he used to sit in his big Windsor chair by the fire, take off his boots and socks and stretch his legs out. This was the signal for Nell and Jennie to sit on the floor, one on either side of his chair, and gently scratch his feet. After a few minutes Father would sigh, pat the girls on the head then go and get ready for his meal.

"Sunny Jim", so called because of his beaming face and angelic nature, was the eldest son. He was not always as angelic as he looked. One day Mother gave all three girls a hard slap across their legs for taking off their boots and stockings on the way home and paddling in the dyke. There was only one way she could have found out about it; Jim must have been telling tales, as George had not been with them that day. The girls vowed revenge.

That night, when they were all upstairs and supposed to be in bed, Alice, Nell and Jennie roused Jim. They made him stand shivering and whimpering in his night shirt in the centre of the cold bedroom. Then, by the light of the one flickering candle Mother allowed them, they stuck pins one by one straight into his night shirt. Poor Jim dare not move. When the girls had finished, blown out the candle and climbed back into bed cuddling their stone hot water bottles, he had to pick out all the pins before he too could get into bed; a bed which was now icy cold. Brothers and sisters could be so cruel, but Jim never told tales again.

George was younger than Jim and went his own way. Despite being the youngest he was usually the ringleader in the children's escapades. He was strong and wiry with a direct gaze, unafraid of owning up when he had done something wrong. A great help to Father from an early age, he hoped to join the Navy when he was old enough. He could tell you where the fox came across the dykes; where the plumpest rabbits had their burrows; how many pheasant chicks were being raised in the copses; which tree the owl roosted in. George was especially fond of ferrets, one of which he nearly always carried in his pocket or stuffed in his shirt front, and of breeding racing pigeons.

None of the brothers and sisters could stand injustices. Nearby, in an old dilapidated cottage, lived elderly Mr. Brown. Mother would cook an extra portion of dinner, and the girls would take it across the lane to him. He pushed an old pram in which he carried his shopping, and all the village boys tormented him, running after him, pulling faces and shouting "prammy Brown, prammy Brown!" The girls were very upset the first time they heard this, and told George. He kept a sharp lookout, and the next time one of the boys jeered at the old man, George set about him with his fists. After that the boys never called Mr. Brown names again, and if George came on the scene they ran away.

The girls were allowed to go in turn with Mother to the market. Father churned the surplus milk into butter in the wooden churn. Mother weighed it into pounds and half pounds, moulded it into square pats with wooden butter hands, wrapped it neatly and put it in her basket. Each farmer's wife had her own distinctive emblem, such as a rose or leaf or cow, on a small wooden wheel which she trundled across or round the side of the butter pat she had made. In this way a customer could recognise the product and buy again from the same person. Alice or Nell collected fresh eggs to take. They loved to put their hands under the warm, motherly, brown hens and carefully lift out from the straw the new-laid eggs. Not Jennie though. She did not like any feathered fowl and could not bear to touch them. Father and the boys would kill, pluck and draw some of the hens for sale and occasionally dig up some vegetables. They would all walk over the fields to wait for the carrier's cart.

A jingling of harness and chattering of voices heralded the arrival of the cart. Mother and her assistant of the day, baskets well laden, clambered onto the cart and under the canvas cover, finding a seat amongst the bevy of farmer's wives exchanging the latest news from different parts of the parish. Before returning home, Mother would give the girls a few coppers to spend. Alice hunted through the shops and stalls for little toys or books for the boys; Nell would buy new hair ribbons for herself and her sisters; Jennie some sweets to share. Then home again in the cart to tell the rest of the family all the news from the market.

4 VISITING AND VISITORS

One of the joys of living in the country was the exciting prospect of visitors coming to stay, or of one of the family going away for a holiday to one of their many relatives. The children took it in turns to visit their grandparents, and, after the postman had delivered the invitation to the child concerned, there was no rest for Mother till she had lifted down from the attic the woven straw bass – a kind of large closed basket. This was packed and unpacked a dozen times before the day of the journey, and sometimes Mother became very exasperated because of the number of treasures the child wished to take.

Alice, of course, had to take her beloved violin as well, and Mother always sent a bag of fresh farm produce for the hostess. George used to grumble as he helped Father carry Alice's luggage to the carrier's cart, but did not mind if it was his turn to go away.

When visiting her maternal grandparents, the carrier took Alice to the railway station, saw to the purchase of her ticket and put her in the charge of the train guard when the train steamed in. The journey was one of the most important parts of the visit, and as Alice sat primly in the guard's van, she would weave silent stories around her situation. Perhaps she was a princess on a visit to another country or a poor orphan child being sent to work for a rich family. Station names were intriguing, and the changing countryside as the train chuffed northwards was fascinating. Instead of flat, open farmland there were hills and valleys, pit heaps and colliery winding gear, huge blast furnaces by the side of the railway, and gaunt chimneys belching clouds of yellow, grey or white smoke into the air. Then, her destination reached, Alice would climb down from the train with her luggage to be met by an aunt, uncle or grandparent.

The children were always made to feel welcome, although the different household routine seemed strange at first. Instead of a flickering candle, the bedroom was lit by a hissing fan-shaped gas jet, hinged on a bracket to the wall. Waking and dressing in the morning was to the accompaniment of the rattling of horses' hooves and cart wheels on the cobbled street outside. Trains passed at regular intervals during the day over the high viaduct near Grandma's house. Sometimes in the night, Alice could hear the distant mournful sound of a train whistle, reminding her of the cry of a forlorn animal in the dark. The streets were lit by gas lamps, and the old lamplighter came round morning and evening with his long pole, using the slow burner at the end to light or extinguish the gas mantle.

The street traders came round, shouting their wares from their carts. Sometimes the muffin man rode down the street. He had a big basket on the front of his bicycle in which he kept the fresh muffins, covered with a spotless white cloth, and he rang a little bell to let the housewives know he was ready for their custom. Alice soon made friends with all the tradesmen. The one she enjoyed watching most of all was the knife grinder. He would cycle down the street with a weird contraption attached to his machine.

"Knives to grind, scissors to mend," he would call, and the lady of the house would bring her blunt knives and scissors for him to sharpen. With his bicycle mounted on a portable stand, the knife grinder would pedal hard driving, a belt which turned his grinding wheel. Holding the blades of knives or scissors at a certain angle against this wheel, he would soon hone them to a fine sharpness.

There was also the "tingle-airy man". He pushed a barrel organ around on a hand cart, stopping here and there to wind a handle. This made the organ play a variety of tunes, to which a sad faced little monkey would dance on top of the organ, then run round the audience with his little red fez cap in his tiny paw for pennies and halfpennies. Alice felt so sorry for the little thing with such an unhappy expression on his wizened face.

It was taken as a matter of course that from an early age you went into town on your own. The different shops and market stalls provided a great deal of choice for spending pocket money and buying little gifts to take back for the rest of the family. Games were played out in the street: hop scotch, whip and top, hide and seek and swinging from a rope on a lamp post. Alice could remember, on one visit, going to play in the local park with her cousins. Their clean, starched pinafores became soiled through rolling down a hill, so Alice and her cousins carefully removed them and washed them in the drinking fountain near the park gates. Alice's aunt was horrified when the girls arrived home trailing their soaking pinafores. After sending Alice to bed for leading her companions astray, she wrote a sharp notice to her sister complaining of Alice's errant ways. The girl did not understand what she had done wrong. She would have been in trouble just as much if she had gone home with a dirty pinafore. Fortunately Mother took no notice of the letter.

"A storm in a teacup," she remarked when Alice was home again.

When any cousins came from the north to stay on the farm, they too found a different world from that of the city. There was unbounded freedom, fresh air and wholesome food, a great variety of things to do, and you could get dirty every day without being in trouble. It always amazed Alice to see pale-faced, spare-fleshed children blossom into brown-skinned sturdy boys and girls. Often the cousins were sent to recover from an illness, and one girl with anaemia responded so well to Mother's treatment – stewed rhubarb and custard every day at tea time – that the doctor was amazed.

Going to stay with Father's parents was a different experience entirely. They too lived in the country, but being older were more set in their ways. Grandpa was very religious. A staunch Methodist, he had a large brass-bound Bible which he kept in a desk in the parlour. Every morning the family and servants had to assemble in the parlour for prayers before the day's work began, and in the evening Grandpa solemnly unlocked the Bible and read a passage from it. As Alice listened to his slow, sonorous reading, she found it hard to reconcile this image with that of a champion skater of Lincolnshire. For that was what he had been in his youth. She tried hard to picture him gliding with the speed of light over the frozen dykes and canals, and she dimly realised what the passage of time meant. Little Grandma Betsy was Grandpa's second wife and ruled her household with a rod of iron. Everything that could be locked up, was; the keys being kept on a chatelaine round her waist. Very short in stature she was always dressed in grey or black, relieving the sombre colour occasionally with a snowy, starched collar or brooch of fashionable Whitby jet.

One of her hobbies was breeding white rabbits. These she killed and skinned; then cured the skins and made bonnets, muffs and mittens with them. The garments were lined with white or red flannel, and whilst the children thought it was a shame the rabbits had to die, they were very glad of the warm presents received at Christmas.

Grandma Betsy

But you had to be so careful when staying at Little Grandma Betsy's. She was so proud of her pure white bed linen that when the children went to bed they had to keep their hands under the bed clothes and the top had to stay un-crumpled. Alice used to wake up fearfully once or twice in the night, hoping the sheet was still as smooth as when she went to sleep. However, all the children thought the best part of all was coming home. First, there was Father, smiling and greeting you at the station with a great big hug, and the ride home in the horse and cart. It was quite surprising how the countryside altered in the time you were away. Next, the welcome into the heart of a loving family, and the recounting of all the happenings. Then, the unpacking and giving of inexpensive but carefully chosen presents, and finally the snuggling down in your own bed with all the well-loved objects and sounds around you.

It was very exciting to see a stranger coming down the lane towards the farm cottage, and the children used to rush out and hang on the gate, trying to identify the caller. Sometimes it would be a tinker, selling or asking to mend pots and pans and household articles. These tinkers travelled throughout the countryside, returning to each farm about once a year. Mother would let the children accompany her to where the tinker had parked his horse-drawn cart. It was an unforgettable sight. Pots, pans basins and kitchen utensils of every sort were hung from any available space, on top, round the sides and underneath the cart. In a sort of cabin in the centre was the living space for the craftsman himself, with a bunk bed and storage space for food. The tinker's tools were usually stored under the body of the four-wheeled cart, along with the horse's food. The horse stood patiently whilst Mother haggled over the price of baking tins or basins, and the children were delighted when she bought something new – though it might only be a bread crock or a moustache cup for Father.

At harvest and threshing time, Irish labourers travelled up and down the country seeking temporary work. Even if Father had nothing to offer them, he would let them sleep in one of the barns or stables, and Mother gave them a hearty breakfast before they left, and sandwiches to help them on their way. After an encounter with the "boyos", the children's conversation was liberally sprinkled with "me darling", "begorrah" and "to be sure now".

The gypsies were visitors that Alice was not too sure about. Were they as friendly as they seemed to be, or as sly as village folk said they were? Father always groaned when he saw the procession of beautifully decorated caravans winding along the country lanes, and Mother gave the children strict instructions not to get too close if they played with the gypsy urchins. Hair was given a thorough going over with a fine tooth comb after the gypsies had departed, and clothes and children an assiduous cleaning. Alice liked to watch the women make flowers from peeled willow twigs, dipping them into various coloured dyes. They also made clothes pegs from pieces of wood, wove baskets from osiers and sold lace and combs. Mother would buy clothes pegs but nothing else

It was fascinating watching the brown-skinned families fit into the wooden caravans. The fittings inside were decorated with pieces of mirrors, glass door knobs, bobble fringe and lace. They were neat and tidy with a place for everything. The gypsies were clever too as they could speak two languages; Romany and English. Alice rather fancied going with them for a while to share their informal way of living, but Nell was terrified, confident that they were going to take her with them and sell her as a slave. George could describe in exact detail how they caught and dressed a rabbit or killed a hedgehog before wrapping it in clay and baking it in the hot coals of their fire. Father was very tolerant of the few turnips, potatoes and eggs they used to take, but breathed a sigh of relief when they departed.

There were other brown-skinned people who visited the farm; gnarled, weather-beaten men living in the woods and carrying on their trade as charcoal burners. Alice and her siblings made friends with these quiet spoken but genuine countrymen. During their sojourn in the woods they built little huts to live in, and peculiar beehive-shaped, hollow-centred ovens. Alice could never understand why the poles used for the ovens did not burn in spite of the high temperatures generated inside as logs were slowly turned into charcoal. In return for some of Mother's generous hospitality, the men stacked logs they did not need in the yard of the farm cottage, so saving the family a lot of hard work sawing wood for the winter.

One summer's day the children came in from school to find a stranger drinking a cool glass of home-brewed beer in the kitchen. He had some very unusual equipment with him: a large square box covered with a piece of black material, three long sticks fastened together at one end and a leather case. As the family gathered round to gaze at him, Mother explained he was a travelling photographer. With true countryside friendliness she had made him a meal, and in repayment he said he would take the family's photograph. Mother and the girls put on clean pinafores, and with much giggling and pushing, the children arranged themselves round Mother outside the cottage door.

The photographer had put the curtain covered box on the three sticks a short distance away, then he hid his head under the curtain several times. Satisfied with the grouping, he admonished them to stay perfectly still whilst he slowly counted to ten. Nothing seemed to happen and Alice felt vaguely disappointed. The photographer departed, thanking Mother for her hospitality and promising to send the picture by post. What excitement when the postman brought the finished print! The children were amazed to see their likeness on the card, but Alice laughed at herself. She looked so sulky as she peeped out from behind her mother's skirts. Alice wished the picture was in colour to show her mother's lovely chestnut brown hair. It was

Mother's only vanity, and Alice loved to watch her combing it each day then plaiting and winding it into a bun at the nape of her neck.

No matter how Alice tried to subdue her own unruly curls, they always escaped confinement and framed her face. Never mind; when she was older she would have a proper studio portrait taken to show what a well-bred lady she had become.

Life was certainly never dull in the country: something always seemed to be happening.

Mother with Alice left, Nell far right and James on Mother's lap

5 ROUND THE KITCHEN FIRE

The kitchen was the focal point of family life. This was the first room where the children played as babies, where they could find Mother ready to listen to their troubles, where they learned to share at mealtimes and where Mother's word was law.

In the farm labourer's cottage was a big cooking range which took up most of one kitchen wall. A fireplace in the centre of the range was flanked on one side by a huge oven with room underneath for hot coals to be pushed in to heat it, and on the other side by a built-in container for heating water. On top of this was a shelf on which to stand pans. The fire itself had a barred hob in front to hold pans of cooking food, and a hook and chain from which a kettle or pan could be suspended over the flames.

Above the fire and oven was a deep shelf for keeping things warm, and over this the mantelpiece. There were various openings all over the range, with little covers which could be removed. These were called flues, and once a week Mother took off the covers and, with a special long handled brush, cleaned out the soot which had collected there. Under the fire was a large ash pan to catch the cinders, and in the hearth a set of fire irons: long-handled brass poker, tongs and shovel. A big brass fender kept the ashes from falling onto the kitchen floor.

The range had to be black-leaded when the fire was out and the oven cold. This was Alice's special job. First she moved the fender and spread protective paper on the enamelled hearth tin, then she fetched the basket with the brushes and dusters in. The liquid black lead was shaken out of the tin onto a soft cloth and spread over the whole black metal surface of the range. With a soft brush she brushed and burnished until the range gleamed and shone. The fire could then be rekindled, and the work of providing food recommenced. Nell abhorred using the black lead, but Alice thought the effort of cleaning the range well worthwhile. It seemed to smile and twinkle at her as if to say "thank you."

In direct contrast to the blackness of the range was the milky whiteness of the large, square kitchen table. This was scrubbed hard every day, and there was really no need for Mother to use a tablecloth – it was so clean. There was a drawer in each side of the table; one for cutlery, towels and dusters; one for table linen and one was Mother's special drawer. Here she kept her household and market accounts, grocery book and purse. The last one was Father's. It contained his betting slips and form books. Everyone had a wooden stool to sit on, which was pushed away under the table when not in use.

Little Grandma Betsy had a similar table in her kitchen, and when any of the children visited her, they put a farthing or halfpenny into the corner of one of the drawers. This was the "magic" drawer, for by the time the child was ready to go home, the small coin had grown into maybe a penny or even a silver threepenny piece. None of the children could understand how this happened. Even George was unable to fathom it out, despite keeping an eye on the drawer for as long as possible on one visit. "Huh! No such thing as fairies," he exclaimed, making sure he had pocketed his coin and was out of earshot of his grandparents.

Below the kitchen window was a stone sink with a tap for cold water. If there was no tap inside a farm worker's cottage then one was out in the yard near the door. Occasionally the water was supplied from a hand pump in the middle of the yard. The boys used to hate this as Father made them go out in all weathers to be washed under it, and carrying water for the house was another chore.

Alice loved to come into the kitchen after school and see her mother busy baking. With sleeves rolled up and wearing a voluminous white apron, she kneaded the bread dough before putting it to rise in front of the fire. There always seemed to be something cooking in the oven; maybe a sheep's head with carrots, turnips, potatoes and pearl barley for a nourishing soup; perhaps a Yorkshire pudding to eat with gravy or cooked with sliced rhubarb and brown sugar as a sweet.

"Never let the Yorkshire pudding batter go up the sides of the basin," warned Mother, "it is very wasteful."

The children's favourite was lardy cake. This was a flat, bread cake baked on the bottom of the oven and eaten warm with butter and treacle. Delicious!

Father's favourite was bread and butter pudding, so thick with fruit and egg custard, that when cold it could be sliced and eaten like a cake.

When any of the hens went off the lay, Father would kill it, pluck and draw it, then bring it in for Mother to cook. Mother would singe off the remaining feathers by turning the bird over the fire, and slowly simmer it for dinner. After dinner the children would take it in turns to share the pulling of the wishbone. Whoever got the longest piece would get their wish – or so they hoped. Sometimes George would bring a rabbit home after he had been out with his ferrets, or Father would shoot a hare for Mother to jug. They had rook pie, which amused Alice. The rooks were skinned not plucked, and when served in a pastry crust with their matchstick like legs sticking out, the children thought they looked very funny.

Cleanliness and godliness ranked equally in Mother's kitchen. No meals were eaten without dirty shoes and mud-splashed clothing first being taken off in the back kitchen, hands thoroughly washed and grace said. No-one was allowed to serve a plate with a splash of gravy on the edge; no elbows could be put on the table, and no-one was allowed to leave the table until Father had finished.

Homemade beer was usually drunk with meals as the water was not necessarily pure. In the spring the children had to gather young green nettles for Mother to brew into nettle beer. The nettles were also eaten as a vegetable, tasting rather like spinach. Rhubarb beer and wine were very refreshing drinks, and Mother made blackberries and elderberries into delicious syrups. Alice and Nell used to soak elder flowers in water and secretly wash in the liquid, hoping to make their freckles disappear and become beautiful.

August and September were the months for mushrooming. The children would go out early into the dew-drenched fields and pick the fungi which had sprung up overnight. After a tasty breakfast of mushrooms and home cured bacon, they would set off for school with a basket of the morning-picked food for the school master.

Although large families were the norm, Mother had to work hard to feed and clothe everyone, as well as clean the house and take care of the pig, hens and cow. The weekly routine rarely varied and there was so much to get into each day. But it was a happy household, and the brothers and sisters enjoyed the responsibility of knowing what they did was appreciated.

A Lincolnshire chapel

Sunday was really a day of rest. When the stock had been fed and the breakfast dishes cleared, the children went upstairs and changed into their best clothes. Then, with dinner simmering in the oven, they walked with Father and Mother to the service at the local chapel. After dinner was eaten and the pots washed up, the children were allowed to play quietly or go for a walk whilst Father slept in his fireside chair and Mother worked on her accounts. At bedtime, Sunday clothes had to be tidied carefully away, and the things they would wear for school on the following day put out.

Monday was washday. In the corner of the back kitchen was a copper – a tank which was filled with water and a fire lit under it. With dolly tub, posser and rubbing board Mother got to work on the laundry: washing, rinsing and wringing the clothes. She used a large wooden-rollered wringer, or mangle as it was called, to squeeze the water out of the washing, but Alice marvelled at how well Mother could wring the clothes with her bare hands. Hardly any water came out of the mangle before the clothes were hung out to dry, either to blow on the line in the yard or dry in front of the fire on the "winter hedge". The wooden clothes' horse was called "the winter hedge" because you could not spread clothes to dry on the hedges in winter as Mother often did in the summer. The ironing was done in the evening with flat irons, which were heated on the hob of the fire. Mother could tell by holding the iron near her cheek if it was hot enough to use, though she taught the girls to spit gently on the hot surface. If the moisture sizzled immediately the iron was ready. George wished he was allowed to iron then he would be able to spit quite legitimately. A dirty iron was rubbed with a bar of soap and pressed over some woollen material to clean it. Mother had several irons heating at the same time: small ones for small items and larger, heavier ones to use on the twill shirts and cord trousers Father wore. A welcome gift for Mother was a home-made iron holder, painstakingly sewn in secret from scraps of material. Wash day had a special clean, steamy smell about it.

On Tuesday the laundry was folded, put away and any repairs done. The girls had to learn to mend their stockings, and Alice was reprimanded when in a fit of pique she said "darn it!"

"Save your darns for your stockings," reproved Mother.

Wednesday was the day when the house was cleaned thoroughly. Windows and furniture throughout the house gleamed and shone, although Mother only used vinegar and water and a chamois leather.

"It's elbow grease that matters," she would say, and George would grit his teeth and rub harder than ever.

The main baking day was Thursday when bread and pies for the following week were made. Mother rarely had to buy any flour, the harvest gleanings being enough to provide for the whole year; the local miller grinding the corn for the villagers. Mmmm, yes, Thursday had a special smell too.

Market day on Friday was a change for Mother and "a change is as good as a rest," was another of her sayings. Up early as usual she would pack the butter Father had churned for her, curds she had made, along with her fruit and pork pies, cakes and curd tarts into her large baskets, then go and wait for the carrier's cart at the end of the lane, accompanied by one of the girls if it was a school holiday. Sometimes she had a wooden stall in the market place and at other times a tarpaulin spread on the cobbles from which she sold her wares. She listened to all the local news, even managing to overhear the farmers' gossip in the local hostelry. Then in the evening when she had settled with her knitting in front of the fire, she would regale Father with all she had heard.

On Saturdays there was a general tidying up and preparations for Sunday. Tasks such as washing up, feeding the farm stock at least once a day, collecting the eggs, cleaning shoes, dusting and black leading were expected to be done without being instructed. Mother was most particular about washing up – each plate, cup or saucer had to be dried separately and left to steam before being stacked away.

Every Saturday night the big tin bath was brought in from the back kitchen and filled with hot water from the tank in the kitchen range. Each child had to have a bath and hair wash before being wrapped in a soft snowy white towel to dry. Father would fall asleep in his big Windsor chair. As his head drooped, eyelids closed and chin became slack, the boys would gaze up at him and say "grunt piggy, grunt piggy, grunt" and sure enough Father would snore. The girls were helpless with laughter, even Mother smiled though she only let it happen once or twice before she mentioned bedtime.

Then off the children had to go. Into the cold bedrooms where their breath came out of their mouths like steam and the windows froze over in winter. But each child knew there was a warm bottle or hot brick wrapped in cosy flannel in the bed to snuggle down with.

Evenings were whiled away sometimes with helping to prick rugs for the cold stone floors of the downstairs rooms. These rag rugs were made with strips of material from clean old clothes which were then pushed down and back up – or pricked – through a piece of heavy sacking. Each child in turn was allowed to draw a pattern to follow on the sacking and, with careful planning, a most colourful rug could be made.

It was comforting on the dark winter evenings to sit round the glowing kitchen fire. There were pictures to be seen in the burning embers, and the children made up stories to fit what they saw: princesses being rescued from burning castles or witches and wizards casting spells in dark hollow caverns. Mother would fetch some of the sweet chestnuts she had gathered in the wood, slit the skins with a knife and put them on the bars of the fire to roast. Sometimes one would burst with a sudden crack, frightening everyone into a fit of nervous giggles.

Alice thought the kitchen was the happiest room in the house and loved it in all its seasons. Although farm life was a never ending round of hard work, there was time for laughter and play. With all the love shown it was a very happy way of living.

6 SUMMER HOLIDAYS

The country year followed the seasons of nature, being ruled by planting, harvest and the length of daylight. Each holiday had its own special appeal; the awakening of the countryside at Easter when the blossoms on the fruit trees flirted in the breeze like a lacy wedding veil, giving promise of delicious fruit in late summer; the muddy back-breaking work of potato picking work in October, scrabbling in the soil for the potatoes turned up by the horse-drawn plough; and the crisp, snowy promise of Christmas.

There were the occasional days of holiday, such as the day when the older school children sat their examination for entrance to the grammar school in the nearby town. Alice was very much in awe of the older girls and worked hard at her lessons, hoping she might succeed one day in going to the grammar school.

May Day was usually a holiday as well. Celebrated in the morning with maypole dancing in the playground or on the village green, the boys and girls first went into the fields or lanes to gather greenery and flowers which were plaited into a crown for the top of the maypole and woven into garlands for the May Queen and her attendants to wear. Alice was never picked to be May Queen, but in turn both Nell and Jennie were chosen.

After dancing round the maypole, intricately weaving the coloured ribbons in and out, the children were free for the rest of the day. Splitting into small groups and dressing up in all sorts of costumes borrowed from parents and grandparents, they formed into little processions and toured the farms and cottages singing "Rule

Britannia" and rattling home-made collecting tins.

Without a doubt, the favourite of all was the long break from school in August. Summer days were very hot, and the children could go barefoot, enjoying the freedom from long stockings and stout leather boots. The sun browned their agile limbs and, once their tasks were done, they could play to their hearts content. Daisy chains and bouquets of wild flowers were made for whoever was the Princess or Queen. Dolls and prams were pushed miles up and down the lanes. The boys raced about bowling iron hoops or pushed each other on trolleys made from wooden boxes and old pram wheels. There were houses to be made in the hay piled high in the barn; swings made from knotted ropes tied to tree branches; pieces of board used as sledges for sliding down grassy slopes; Mother's old clothes line cut up for skipping ropes. And all the time the sun beamed down from a cloudless blue sky.

The Sunday School treat took place in the summer holidays. The Prize Giving had taken place one Sunday in July, and each child who had regularly attended chapel during the previous year had received a small leather bound Bible with his or her name written inside in beautiful, copperplate handwriting. But now the excitement was intense. Gone was the quiet decorum of Sunday mornings, although all the village children were dressed in their best clothes. The boys were in knee-length breeches, long socks, jackets, shirts and caps; the girls in starched white dresses with lace-edged petticoats, long black stockings and wide-brimmed, ribbon-trimmed hats. Nell suffered agonies the night before the treat, with her hair in rags so that she could have long ringlets hanging down over her shoulders. Mother would get some narrow strips of calico, wind a lock of hair with a strip of calico tightly together round her finger then tie a knot in the calico. If she pulled a little too hard and Nell complained, Mother would say dryly "Pride's painful," or "what can't be cured must be endured." However Nell obviously thought it was worth it.

Farmers of the district supplied the horses and carts to take all the children to the valley where the treat was to be held. Alice was so proud when Father led his horses and cart up to the chapel. She was sure their jingling brasses shone more brightly and their coats were glossier than any of the others. When all the children were seated on the carts, the procession moved through the village and down the winding lane to one of the local beauty spots, a narrow grassy valley. The happy, beaming children sang all their favourite hymns on the way, and on arrival each child was given a white paper bag containing a couple of sticky iced buns and two sandwiches. The Sunday School teachers organised races, and Alice, who ran nearly everywhere, was off like the wind to take part.

Children fell down in the grass, fell out with each other, fell over their feet in the races, and if there were any puddles, fell in. Chubby Sunny Jim spent nearly all the day toiling up the steep grassy slopes of the valley then rolling over and over down to the bottom in a rush, shrieking with delight as he tottered dizzily about. A good time was had by all, and at the end of the day, as the cart loads of tired, sticky grubby children were driven back to the village, no-one cared how they looked. White dresses were green with grass stains, and Nell's hair was as straight as nature intended.

Harvest came at the end of the summer holidays. The children

Haymaking in Victorian times

would help Father lead the horses down to the fields with the reaping machine harnessed behind. Whilst Father cut the corn or barley, other farm workers followed behind, tying the corn into sheaves with twisted straws. When a field had been cut, the sheaves were piled into stooks – like little tents – so that the wind could blow through and dry the grain. Sometime during the morning the girls would go back home to help Mother carry the big baskets of food and drink for all the harvesters. At dinner time everyone stopped work and came and sat in the shelter of the hedge. The men wore hats to shield them from the sun, and the ladies and girls pretty coloured cotton sun bonnets with a frill at the back to shade the neck. In the baskets were hot meat pies, home boiled ham, cheese and crusty bread, with bottles of cold tea or home brewed beer to quench thirsty throats. Then it was time to move on to the next field. So it went on whilst

Threshing the grain

ever there was any daylight left, till all the corn was cut, bound and stooked.

Once the corn was judged to be dry enough to be threshed, it was pitchforked onto carts and led to await the huge steam driven engine which toured the farms providing power for the threshing machines. The corn was fed into the machine, the grain threshed out into sacks, and the straw piled in the barn for winter bedding for the cattle.

The boys liked this part best. All the available menfolk and boys gathered round with sticks and pitchforks at the ready, and terrier dogs waiting to pounce on, shake and kill the rats which were hiding in the corn sheaves. The noise was deafening, and Alice was sure that, if she had been a rat, she would have been frightened to death by the hullabaloo and clamour. George was very proud when he first hit a rat (more by good luck than good judgement) though Mother stopped him telling all the gory details at the tea table.

"I'll tell you all about it later," he promised Sunny Jim who could not eat his tea fast enough.

The village chapel was decorated for Harvest Thanksgiving, when everyone sang the lovely harvest hymns, then tucked into the Harvest Supper. The womenfolk tried to outdo each other in the presentation of their contributions, and Alice thought the supper table looked an absolute picture.

When the corn had been led from the fields, the farm workers and their families could go gleaning. This meant picking up all the loose ears and grains of corn left in the fields after the crop had gone to the stackyard. Sharp eyes and nimble fingers were needed, and the grain thus gathered was for the use of the farm workers and would be ground into flour for them by the village miller. After harvest the boys would help Father burn the stubble in preparation for the autumn ploughing and seeding of the winter wheat. The crackling flames lit up the sky luridly like a red sunset, and the smell of burning lingered on clothes and hair.

The early apples and plums were ready towards the end of the holidays, and George was able to exercise his climbing skills quite legitimately. Alice had her eyes on the late cherries ripening on the row of tall trees forming one of the farm boundaries. She waited until Mother had no further tasks for her to do, then quietly slipped away. Climbing with a skill equal to her brothers', she was soon in the upper branches, settling herself against the tree trunk and gorging on the delicious fruit. She ate greedily until almost replete, then her feast was interrupted by Mother calling the children in for tea. Hurriedly descending from her perch she washed the cherry stains from her mouth and hands and went in for her meal.

Appetites were usually robust and Mother glanced anxiously at her eldest daughter as she only picked at her food.

"Try a little pudding Alice," she suggested "it's your favourite, cherry pie." Alice groaned, gulped, then ran from the table. After spending a miserable night being sick, she got very little sympathy.

"Serve you right," said Mother, and Alice did not eat cherries again.

Each village church or chapel had its own small burial ground. Alice felt very sorry for some of the people buried in the church yard nearest to their homes. Some graves were tiny with only a plain stone at the head. Other tombstones were more ornate with statues of angels or replicas of urns. One of her favourite holiday tasks was to

take a bucket of water and scrubbing brush to the church yard and donning her apron she would scrub away at the green lichen stains on the gravestones, singing hymns to herself, much to the amusement of passers-by. The tranquillity of the surroundings was very soothing to the girl after the hustle and bustle of family life.

It was back to school after the summer break, to work through the long weeks before Christmas. Days grew shorter, nights colder, and when she looked up at the brilliant stars on a clear frosty night, Alice felt a great air of expectancy; almost as if the whole world was holding its breath for the great celebration. There was very little money with which to buy Christmas gifts. Indeed the children did not expect much. They always tried to make presents for each other, and woe betide anyone who tried to take a peep into a hidden box. But before Christmas there was another annual event in the farm calendar: pig killing time.

7 THE SALTING TROUGH

Nell and Jennie pushed the doll's carriage down the lane. They had been very busy on this unexpectedly warm and sunny autumn morning washing their dollies' clothes. The little girls had rubbed the clothes well with the hard green soap Mother used. Scrubbing hard with the clothes brush, rinsing and wringing out had made them hot and flushed. Mother had fastened a small clothes line for them across a corner of the yard, and the girls had enjoyed a cool glass of nettle beer after pegging the clothes on the line. The small garments had soon dried, and now dressed again, the dolls were sitting in the pram.

George raced past them, closely followed by his shadow, little Jim. They were trundling their iron hoops, guiding them with metal hooks. As the hoops ran faster down the lane so did the boys.

"We're going to the salting trough," shouted George.

"Come on," panted Jim, trying hard to catch George. "We'll play pirates."

Alice came skipping down the lane, her rope, made from a piece of old washing line, whirling round in time with her nimble feet. Nell and Jennie hurried on. Games involving the salting trough were usually exciting, wet and muddy.

This trough, a wide shallow wooden bath, was kept moist in the stream, then taken out and used for salting and curing the sides of bacon and ham after pig killing time in October.

At the bottom of the lane curved the lazily flowing stream. Long strands of green water weed dotted with starry white flowers provided cool cover for the minnows and sticklebacks suspended almost motionless in the water, facing the current, waiting for food. Water boatmen, busy beetle-like creatures, skated along on the smooth surface of the water. Dragonflies hovered, their iridescent wings shimmering in the sun before they darted into the sedges and rushes growing on the banks of the stream.

Near the wooden plank bridge some willow branches bent low, the leafy tips dipping gently into the water. If you were very quiet for a while you could hear the occasional "plop" as a frog jumped into the stream or the subdued "quack" of an idly paddling duck.

The children gathered together on the banks of the stream.

"What are we going to do today?" asked the girls.

"I know," said George, eyeing the dolls in their spotless finery, "let's have Moses in the bulrushes."

"Ooh, yes," agreed everyone, the Bible story fresh in their minds from Sunday School.

"We need a basket," said Alice.

"And a bucket to empty the salting trough with," added Jim.

"And one of Mother's clothes props so's we can use the trough as a boat," chimed in Nell.

"Let's go and fetch the things then," suggested Alice, and leaving the dolls and hoops on the grass they trudged back to the cottage. Carrying an old egg basket, a prop and an old piece of net curtain in which to swaddle one of the dolls, they were soon down by the stream again. There, they took off boots, socks and stockings before bailing out the trough.

The water felt deliciously cool to their feet after the hot confinement of wool and leather. Whilst George and Jim used the bucket to empty the vessel, the girls gathered bunches of buttercups, daisies and tasselled grasses with which to decorate the basket. Jennie made a daisy chain which she wound round her curtain-swathed doll who was then tenderly placed in the basket.

"Right," said George, taking charge, "are we ready?"

The others nodded agreement.

"Nell, you're Miriam putting the basket in the water and hiding to see when the baby is found. Jim and I will pole the boat. Alice, you be the king. And Jennie, you're the king's daughter who finds the baby."

With much pushing and shoving, splashing and heaving, the heavy trough was moved slowly into the middle of the stream. Standing precariously in the centre of the trough, Alice tried to think of herself as regal; a noble monarch in that far-off land all those years ago. It was difficult to keep her footing as the trough tilted and swayed; Jennie, with sense and discretion, sat on the damp boards clinging to the sides.

Nell had retreated to the shade of a clump of willows after placing the basket in the stream. Slowly the trough was poled towards the drifting babe, George manfully trying to steer a straight course with the one pole, and Jim darting from side to side in response to his brother's shouted instructions. Nell watched anxiously from the bank. The royal barge was gradually moving nearer to the basket with its precious cargo. Unfortunately the eddies and currents created by George's strenuous manoeuvres swirled the basket into the middle of the stream, and before the children in the salting trough could catch it, the babe had begun floating downstream out of their reach.

"Oh," wailed Jennie. "Catch it Nell. Oh, it's my best doll. Hurry George!"

George's face grew red with the effort of poling faster. Nell pushed her way out of the willow branches and ran along the bank to keep up with the basket. Alice moved into the front of the trough-cum-boat, vainly trying to reach the doll, and Jim began rocking the trough and shouting in his excitement.

It was all too much. With a sickening lurch the trough tipped to one side and the children were deposited in the stream. With loud shrieks, Alice and Jennie floundered in the cold but fortunately shallow water, whilst George and Jim, the former silent with rage, the latter silent with fright, stumbled after them to the opposite bank of the stream.

The dripping, bedraggled little group stood shivering there, Jennie crying bitterly. On the other side Nell was gesticulating urgently. Following her gestures the children saw the basket with the sweetly smiling doll had come to rest by the wooden bridge lower down the stream. It was slowly sinking and Jennie wailed louder than ever as she saw her beloved doll gradually go under the water.

"I'll get it," shouted Nell and, tucking her full skirts into her knickers, she bravely paddled into the stream to rescue the doll.

The forlorn little group moved slowly over the bridge, along the bank of the stream and trailed up the lane to the cottage. Gone were the crisply starched white aprons; petticoats and trousers sagged wetly around chilled limbs; wet hair clung damply to woebegone faces. Mother would be very cross when she saw all their wet and dirty clothes. But the punishment meted out by her would be light indeed; for who would explain to Father how the salting trough came to be marooned much further down the stream on the other side.

8 PIG KILLING TIME

"You can use every bit of a pig but its squeak," said Mother.

It was autumn. The hours of daylight were fewer, evenings darker and nights colder. Often, on waking in their cold bedrooms, the children could see their breath in clouds of steam, and the windows were painted with dainty fern-like patterns. Dressing was a cold and shivery business, little fingers finding buttons and laces difficult to fasten.

Breakfast in the warm kitchen, with Father's home-cured bacon sizzling in the frying pan sending a lovely aroma wafting through the door, made one feel ready to face whatever the day might bring. In the daytime the bright autumn sun shining from clear cloudless skies marked the trees, hedges, dykes and building in superb detail.

The first frosts brought the leaves tumbling from the trees, and as the children scrunched their way home from school through a carpet of golden brown, the boys collected caps full of horse chestnuts ready to thread on string and play "conkers". Father showed the boys how to soak the best conkers in vinegar and bake them in the oven so they would be very tough and win the championship.

The girls collected acorns to give to the pig – the huge pink, bristle skinned animal – who had been part of their lives during most of the year. Ever since the early spring day when Father's employer gave them the skinny, squealing piglet to fatten for their own use, Alice and Nell had taken charge. They had swept the cobwebs and rubbish out of the pig sty; laid a covering of warm straw on the floor;

scrubbed the food trough till Mother said it was as clean as her best china tea service; and then diligently looked after their pet. After much deliberation he had been called Snuffles, for when picked up and cuddled, he would bury his snout under Alice's arm and snuffle away.

Snuffles was fed twice a day. When Mother or Father had finished churning butter, they would drain off the buttermilk, and Alice or Nell would carry the bucket of liquid down to the sty. Mixed with some pig meal this was very good for Snuffles and, along with household scraps, cabbages or cauliflower leaves and small pig potatoes for food, he developed well.

Mucking out was a job no-one relished, but it had to be done. Jennie flatly refused, turning up her dainty little nose in disgust, but Alice and Nell soldiered on. Sometimes, when the sty was cleaned and before fresh straw was spread, the girls got a pail of water and a scrubbing brush and gave Snuffles a good wash. He loved that and lay on his side, snuffling and grunting with pleasure. Afterwards, as he stretched out contentedly on a dry bed of straw, the girls would sit on the wall of the sty, idly scratching his back with a long stick and comment favourably on their handiwork.

"You know Alice, he's bigger than Mr. Jones's pig."

"Yes, and isn't he a lovely colour?"

"I love the way his ears bend over."

"He's very intelligent isn't he Nell? I'm sure he knows we're talking about him," and the large, pink animal would snuffle his approval, blinking his little blue eyes with their soft golden lashes.

Beaming with satisfaction, the girls sauntered up to the farm cottage to be met by Father.

"Well girls, it's time to fetch the salting trough."

Alice and Nell exchanged anguished glances. They knew what that meant! The salting trough was a wide, shallow wooden vessel into which the sides and joints of pork were put and rubbed with salt and nitre as part of the curing process. Except when needed at pig killing time it was kept in the shallow boundary stream so that it did not dry out. The children spent many happy hours playing in it during the summer. It was used as a punt with a whippy willow wand as a pole; a pirate ship with the girls being made to walk the plank; a lifeboat with pieces of wood for oars and Alice or Nell pretending to be Grace

Darling and rescuing the boys from dire peril; and as a tank for keeping the frog spawn, minnows and sticklebacks found in the stream.

So the time they had dreaded had come. Snuffles was to fulfil his preordained destiny and provide meals for the growing family. No use protesting, but Alice and Nell could eat nothing more that day, Jennie joining in their silent sorrow.

Saturday, pig killing day, dawned fine and clear. Alice wished it could have rained to mingle with her inward tears. Mother, understandingly sent her daughters with a basket of freshly gathered mushrooms to one of the elderly ladies who lived beyond the farm. As the girls glumly set off, the boys, bustling with importance, donned sacking aprons and followed Father to the shed where he had honed his knives to a razor-edged sharpness. Walking down the lane, the girls could hear the squeals as the huge pig was pulled from his pen seeming to know his fate,

"Don't go so fast Ally," wailed Jennie as the older girls quickened their pace. Alice and Nell looked at each other, eyes bright with unshed tears.

"It's a long way" said Alice gruffly, swallowing a lump in her throat. Nell sniffed hard then wiped the back of her hand over her eyes. Sensing something of her sisters' grief, Jennie stopped complaining and tried to make her little legs move more quickly, until at last they were away from the farm cottage and out of earshot.

The girls dawdled home, filling their now empty basket with late blackberries and cob nuts from the hedgerows, and trying to put off the moment of arrival when they would have to walk past the empty sty.

When they were back at the cottage the deed was done. The pig was dead, strung up by its back legs with a large bucket under its head to catch the blood from where Father had cut its throat. Everyone had to help deal with the carcass, and it would be nearly two weeks before everything was finished. Father slit down the belly of the pig and its innards were removed. The intestines were emptied then boiled, ready to be used as sausage skins; heart, liver, kidneys and sweetbreads separated to be used in various ways; and the meat was ready to be cut into different joints.

The children were busy carrying pails of boiling water for Mother to use as she scraped the bristles off the skin. They had to put the trotters and part of the head into a pan on the fire to stew gently before being finely chopped, seasoned, and ladled into basins to set as brawn. The pig's cheeks were scored, the rind rubbed with salt and roasted in the oven for tea; the tongue boiled then rolled and pressed ready for a special occasion. Both sides of the animal were rubbed with various salts and herbs to begin the curing process for bacon. These, along with two hams from the legs, were put in the salting trough.

Curing ham and bacon took a long time, with a lot of attention being paid to the rubbing in. Each housewife had her own special mixture of herbs, but Alice thought the smell of her family's bacon frying in the pan was almost a delicious meal in itself. At bedtime the girls were so tired that they were asleep before they had time to brood over the demise of their pet. There was a lot to do on the Sunday, and for once the family did not attend Chapel or Sunday School. The meat had to be dealt with as soon as possible. Half of the meat was put through the mincing machine and blended with herbs for sausages. The nimble fingers of the girls were occupied filling the freshly cleaned guts with sausage meat till they were airtight and would keep for a long time. Then, whilst the girls chopped some of the remaining meat into small pieces, Mother made some hot water pastry which she moulded into pie shapes and put into a big oven dish. These she filled with the chopped meat, a pastry lid was put on and the pies baked slowly in the oven. Simmering on the hob were some of the rib and leg bones of the pig to make stock. When the pies were cooked, Mother cleared the scum from the surface of the stock and poured some of this liquid into the pies through a small hole she had left in the pastry lid. When the pies were full they were carried carefully onto the stone slab in the larder and left to cool. The stock set like jelly, forming an airtight seal, and the pies kept sweet and wholesome for months.

Farm and home chores had to be attended to as usual, but Father found time to carve the remainder of the pork into chops, steaks and joints, most of which would be preserved in brine. Fat was cut into small pieces and blended with the pig's blood and herbs for black pudding. A lot of fat was rendered in the oven, the liquid solidifying into pure lard. The crunchy scraps left over were sprinkled with salt and pepper and stored in an earthenware jar to be eaten later with various savoury dishes. One of Mother's specialities was brain sauce, considered a delicacy, and served with triangles of thin crisp toast. Any leftover bits of the carcass were simmered for stock or dripping.

At last all was finished. Reconciled to the loss of their pig, the girls shared Mother's glow of satisfaction and achievement when they looked in the back kitchen and the keeping cellar at the flitches of bacon, ham, joints of meat and strings of sausages hanging from the hooks in the ceiling rafters. Also the rows of pies, black puddings, basins of brawn and jars of lard, dripping and fat-sealed stock which were permanently cool on the stone slabs every cottage had in the cellar and larder.

To celebrate the end of all the extra hard work, Mother cooked a joint of belly pork, rubbing the skin with salt so that it turned into lovely brown crackling. How the children relished the flavour and crunchiness, although Alice, surreptitiously catching Nell's eye as they each held a piece of succulent crackling in their fingers, had a fleeting feeling of guilt at so enjoying the food provided by Snuffles.

"Never mind Alice," said George, with a wicked glint in his eye, "you can have another pig for a pet next year." Nell kicked him hard on his shin under cover of the table, but George just smirked and carried on with his meal. That evening at bedtime he bade the girls a cheery goodnight. As they undressed by candlelight Alice glanced round. George had been too good. It was unusual for him not to hit back. Nell, ever precise, neatly folded her clothes for the morning and then slipped her hands under the counterpane to warm them on the hot, flannel-wrapped brick Mother had earlier placed on the feather filled mattress.

"Let's fold the sheet back Alice," she suggested, and then you can blow out the candle." Suiting the action to the words, the girls lifted the crisply laundered sheet from the pillow.

Nell shrieked as she recoiled in horror, then ran gasping to the slop bucket to be violently sick. Alice took one look at what lay revealed and realised why George had been so smug. He had got his own back after all. There, nestling in the centre of Nell's pillow staring glassily upwards, was the unblinking, blood encrusted eye of Snuffles, their pig.

9 CHRISTMAS

At last Christmas time drew near. Soft spring days, warm summer evenings, glowing autumn colours – all seemed distant memories in the here and now crispy, crackling world of winter. Some days the children had to struggle to school in the icy winds which blew over the flat fields and dykes; a wind which always seemed to blow into their faces whichever way they going. At other times, wispy grey strands of fog hid the familiar path and landmarks of trees, and posts loomed out of their shrouds like silent monsters. The spiders' webs were hung with dewdrop diamonds, and George and Jim broke small forked twigs to twist into the bejewelled gossamer.

On the hard bright frosty mornings, it was great fun sliding on the frozen puddles in the wheel ruts made by carts in the lane. Entry to the sluice gates was barred by long pointed icicles, glinting and gleaming in the rose-red winter sun. The skeletons of the leafless trees stood out starkly against the clear cold sky, and down by the stream the pollarded willows looked like gnarled old men with spiky limbs and white rimed hair.

Although lessons in most subjects were not allowed to lapse, the excitement mounting in the children at the approaching festival could not be hidden, and the preparations for decorating the schoolroom went ahead. Paper was coloured and cut into fancy chains, snowflakes and snowmen decorated the windows, and paper lanterns were strung around the schoolroom. The big iron stove in the middle of the room, which warmed both classes, was kept well stoked up, and everyone sat as near as possible to the brass-railed fire guard.

"We shall be having our Nativity tableaux as usual," said the schoolmaster one morning when the children were assembled in rows before him, "and everyone will be taking part." The girls were thrilled but several of the boys pulled faces. George grumbled all the way home that day as they trudged across the snow sprinkled fields. Alice, Nell and Jennie tried to cheer him up by singing all the carols and Christmas songs they were learning, but it was no use. Practises went ahead at school, the children having to remain motionless in their particular tableau whilst there was a reading from the Bible or a carol. The older girls helped to wash and alter the costumes which were stored throughout the year in a huge wicker basket. The three sisters had become quite inured to George's protests about taking part and, on the day of the final rehearsal, as they walked to school, they failed to notice the spring in George's step and the cherubic smile on Sunny Jim's face.

The rehearsal began well but there was a noticeable stirring among the boys.

"Boys be still," commanded the schoolmaster. The tableau froze and all was well again until the final moment when the plump, solemn faced, blonde haired, blue eyed angel raised her hands in blessing. Glancing down she gave a piercing shriek and, jumping down from the stage, ran crying to the cloakroom. The teaching assistant hurried out to calm the stricken angel, and the schoolmaster strode up the hall to where the shepherds were kneeling. Broad grins on their faces as they looked at George, gave the game away.

"Please sir, I'm sorry sir," said George. "It was Ferdie sir. I had to have him in my pocket to keep warm, and he ran and nipped her ankle." The stern faced teacher seized George by the scruff of the neck and hauled him off to suffer a stroke of the cane on the seat of his brown serge knickerbockers. One thing about George, he took his punishment like a man, but Jennie burst into tears and Alice and Nell exchanged anguished glances. The indignity of it.

The main performance however went off without a hitch, and as the family walked back to the cottage through the starlit night, there seemed to be an air of quiet expectancy about the countryside, almost as if nature was holding its breath waiting for Christmas morning.

Life had been very busy in Willowgarth cottage with so much

preparation to be done before the great day. During the preceding months, Mother had fattened a goose for Christmas dinner, and it had become quite a character in the farmyard, chasing anyone or anything if there was the slightest chance of a nibble of food. Father having killed and plucked it, the goose was now stuffed and ready for the oven. Alice had begged some of the soft goose down from her Father and had made a little pillow for Jennie's doll's pram as her Christmas present. The boys had taken some of the long quills from the wings of the goose and, under Father's watchful eye, used their knives to make pens for Grandfather and Grandmother. The children wrinkled their noses at the awful smell as Mother singed the last traces of feathers from the bird.

The carefully-made plum puddings were waiting to be steamed again. Everyone had had a hand in making them. One Saturday, sitting round the spotlessly clean kitchen table, the children had stoned all the raisins and currants before Mother washed and dried them. The boys chopped the suet whilst the girls peeled and shredded the carrots. Then, when all the ingredients were mixed together, each member of the family had had a wish and a stir, before Mother wrapped a silver threepenny piece in greaseproof paper and dropped it into the mixture. Someone would be lucky at Christmas dinner time. The mixture was portioned out into basins which were then tied in pudding cloths and steamed for several hours. When cold, they joined the pork pies and basins of brawn on the stone slab in the pantry. Similar preparations had taken place before the Christmas cake and mince pies were ready. Mother rewarded her helpers with a lump of fruity tasting sugar from the candied peel when they had finished. What a heady smell of brandy there was in the back kitchen where the mincemeat was soaking in an old bread crock, waiting to be spooned into stone jars!

The apples for the mincemeat had been fetched from the smaller of the two attics. Mother and Alice exchanged rueful glances when the former mentioned she needed some apples bringing down.

One Sunday in autumn, Alice had torn her best petticoat. She had been chasing George, determined to make him stop teasing his sisters and, in climbing after him into the hay loft, had caught her undergarment on a nail. The boys had chortled with glee when she had to go in and show the damage to Mother. Not that it was such a heinous crime, but it happened to be Sunday when boisterous games were frowned upon and Little Grandma Betsy had come to tea. Under her disapproving eye, Mother had sent Alice upstairs to sit in the apple room until forgiven.

Carefully picked in the autumn, the apples were kept in the second attic across the landing from the room where Alice practised her violin so diligently. Feeling very mutinous for being, as she thought, unjustly punished, the young girl sat on the floor and gazed at the fruit stored in the tiny room under the eaves. The apples were spread round the room on open wooden laths so as not to become bruised by touching each other, and they smelt delicious. Some were rosy red eating apples, others large green cookers, and would provide fruit all through the winter. Alice got up and walked round, examining them as she had seen her Mother do to make sure they were without blemish.

"One rotten apple will spoil a whole barrelful," Mother had said. Feeling hungry, for she had missed tea, Alice reached out to pick a large eating apple from the back row, knocking two or three others onto the floor as she did so. Rather over ripe they smashed onto the floor, and Alice slipped as she tried to move away. An idea came into her mind as she saw the smashed fruit, and she spread the pulp along the floor, rubbing it smooth with the leather sole of her boot. When it was slippery enough for her satisfaction she had a lovely time sliding up and down, and what had been meant as a punishment, turned into a game. Mother did not use the apple room for banishment any more.

Now the apples were peeled, cored and diced before being mixed with the other ingredients and a liberal measure of brandy stirred in.

One wintry night, when the fire was blazing well, the children sat round the table and laboriously wrote their letters to Santa Claus. These were then put carefully in the fire and watched closely to see what happened. If the letters came down the chimney then the asked-for presents would not materialise, but as the family waited with baited breath all the papers curled into flame and wafted up the chimney with the smoke. Requests for presents were very modest, the children having the whole of nature outside their door to play with. There had been furtive journeys to secret places where surprise presents were being prepared. Even George had made a gift for everyone.

At last it was Christmas Eve. The village band, warmly dressed with scarves holding down their navy gold-braided caps and with overcoats on top of their smart serge jackets, played at various points in the parish. The mitten-protected fingers of the bandsmen did their best to play in the cold winter night by the light of lanterns carried on long poles by young sons and daughters. The whole family put on their warmest clothes to go and listen at the end of the lane. The sound of music carrying through the clear frosty air sent icy tingles up and down Alice's spine. Other farming families from the scattered cottages joined in singing the carols, and the country doctor, riding home from a late call, reined in and added his voice to the happy music makers. Back in the cosy kitchen, sleepy but excited, the children had a warm drink before going up to bed. Each child took one of their long woollen stockings and pegged it onto the foot of the bed, silently hoping it would be full in the morning.

George was the first to wake. He hopped out of the warm cocoon of his feather mattress, shivered his way to the foot of the brass bedstead and felt at the stocking he had left hanging there.

Yes! It was full with all sorts of interesting bumps and bulges. He shook Sunny Jim awake and together they carefully carried their treasures through to their sisters' bedroom. The girls woke instantly, and as they all snuggled into the big bed Nellie and Jennie shared, Alice crept downstairs for a light for the candle. By its glow they were able to see that Santa had indeed been, and all the stockings stretched and bulged. Although their breath came in frosty clouds, the children kept warm with excitement and anticipation.

"We will each open a present," decreed Alice.

"Please let me start," piped Jim and the others nodded in agreement. What rustling of paper there was as gradually the contents of the parcels were revealed, to the accompaniment of cries of delight and "oohs" and "ahs" of satisfaction. Lovely silky fur bonnets for the girls, warmly lined with white flannel; soft woollen knitted socks and gloves for the boys; a favourite marble generously given by one brother to another; dainty pincushions and dressing table tidies lovingly sewn by little fingers; new hair ribbons, skipping ropes, penknives; nuts and sweets; and, at the bottom of each stocking, a shiny red apple, juicy orange and a bright new penny. Wealth indeed!

Alice particularly liked a ring her grandmother had sent for her. A small gold band decorated with silver ivy leaves in its own velvet case; it just fitted her middle finger. Nell cast covetous eyes on it, and Alice was not in the least surprised when her sister asked if she could wear it that day.

By this time Father had gone downstairs and lit the fire. Mother had prepared breakfast, so the children dressed and tidied their bedrooms. They wished their parents a Happy Christmas and proudly produced the gifts they had made for them. When the dinner preparations were finished and the goose was slowly roasting in the big fireside oven, the outside chores done, and the stock fed, the children walked up the lane to meet their grandparents. The clip-clop of hooves and the rattle of wheels heralded their arrival in the gig, and whilst the girls had a ride, the boys tried to race the vehicle back to the cottage.

Presents were duly displayed and admired, then it was time for dinner. Mother's best snowy white cloth was spread over the table and the places set. Whenever Mother shook out the cloth the children held their breath and watched anxiously. What was it Little Grandma Betsy had solemnly stated?

"If there's a diamond fold in the centre of the cloth it means a death in the family."

But once again the cloth had been folded correctly and everything was alright.

Father carved the golden brown goose, the newly sharpened knife cutting through the crisp skin as if it were butter. The aroma, as the fat and juices ran down the plump bird to collect in the hollow at the end of the large dish, made the children's mouths water. Each was wondering if they would be lucky enough to get some of the meat they liked best: Jennie, the sweet breast; Nell and Jim the juicy thigh; Alice and George a bone to pick with their strong teeth. Mother dished the vegetables into tureens which matched the blue and white pattern of the meat dish, dinner plates and gravy boat. There were sprouts, carrots, turnips and potatoes, all from Mother's garden, garnished with white sauce and rich brown gravy.

When everyone was served, eyes were closed, heads bowed and grace said. Alice was sorry that plum pudding followed the savoury dishes on Christmas Day. She was usually so full of the first course that she had to refuse dessert, remembering with chagrin the time she had left her pudding practically untouched.

"We have someone whose eyes are bigger than her stomach," Grandma had remarked caustically. Jim had gazed at Alice in awe, expecting her eyes to grow larger by the minute. This time she was able to eat a small portion of the brandy-flamed pudding but without the rum sauce so favoured by the adults. To Nell's delight - and George's disappointment - she found the silver coin in her helping of pudding. With Grandma Betsy's beady eyes on him, George did not dare voice his thoughts.

When all was cleared away and Mother had poured into basins the fat which had rendered out of the goose – to rub on chests to ease winter coughs among other things – the children were ready to play games. Christmas was of the few occasions when the parlour was used, and Father had lit a fire in that room. The well-polished furniture gleamed in the flickering firelight, and everyone was on their best behaviour until the games got under way. Old favourites such as "I spy", "Apple, apple, apple" ,"Animal Dumbo", "I am a Cobbler" and "Charades" were interspersed with songs, violin solos and recitations. Father got out his concertina and everyone joined in the carols he played. It seemed to be teatime in a flash. The table was reset with the Christmas cake as the centre piece, and although everyone had been replete after dinner, goodly portions of pork pie, tongue, pickles, cake and cheese were disposed of. Alice was very proud of the wafer thin slices of bread and butter Mother cut on special occasions and every Sunday teatime. She had eventually mastered the art herself but not before she had cut many strange-shaped slices.

All too soon it was time for Grandpa and Grandma to make the journey home. Well wrapped up in a beautiful rabbit fur cloak she had made herself, Little Grandma Betsy was nearly hidden from sight in the gig. Grandpa lit the candles in the bullseye lanterns on the outside of the shafts, climbed into the driving seat, and with a crack of the whip they were away.

The bright moon sailed through the serene sky lighting up the snowy landscape till it seemed almost as bright as day. Myriads of stars hung like lanterns above their heads. Yawning prodigiously the children slowly went inside and with no fuss or protestations went up to bed.

"You won't need any rocking tonight," remarked Mother as she tucked them into bed and the children smiled drowsily as they went to sleep.

10 A GREAT CHANGE

The family had been at Willowgarth for quite a long time when Father decided to try his luck in town. When his contract expired, he left his job on the farm and obtained work as a carter. This entailed taking large consignments of goods on horse drawn carts from either the railway station or canal staithe, to the factories or mills in town. It was very exciting for the children as trunks were packed with clothes and linen for despatch by rail to the town. Grandma had arranged for the family to rent a terrace house near where she lived, and several aunts and uncles had cleaned and painted the house ready for occupation.

When, tired and hungry, they eventually arrived at the new house, they found the accommodation was a room and kitchen, keeping, coal and wash cellars underneath, two bedrooms on the first floor and an attic room up a second flight of stairs. The three girls were to sleep in the attic whilst the boys and Mother and Father had the other two bedrooms. Various pieces of furniture had been donated by other members of the family, and the house seemed warm and welcoming with a cheery fire burning in each of the two downstairs rooms. Grandma was waiting with a hot meal for them – some of her delicious stew, which she served with dainty triangles of toast. The children quickly went to sleep, looking forward to exploring further tomorrow. What a surprise they got when they went to the outside lavatory next morning! It was built onto the house and had a piped water supply so that, when you had finished, you only needed to pull a wooden handle on a chain, and a shower of water came down a pipe and flushed away the waste. What luxury! The wooden door could also be bolted from the inside for privacy, and Nell soon learned to disappear there after a meal and so escape having to do the washing up. This went on for quite a while till George finally got tired of having to dry the pots. Near Bonfire Night, he bought one or two jumping crackers, lit one and pushed it under the door when Nell was sitting on the pot. Her screams brought Mother rushing out, and although George felt the flat of her hand on his chubby legs it was worth it to get Nell back to washing up again.

It was very strange attending a school that was just around the corner, where lessons and playtime were accompanied by the rumble of trains passing over the viaduct adjacent to the playground. Instead of green grass to play on, there was the tarred surface of the playground or the cobblestones of the street. New friends had to be made, and the children were glad they had brothers and sisters in school for mutual support. Being able to go home for the midday meal was a bonus, as it made a welcome break in the day. Alice was able to continue with her violin lessons and practised in the attic. At the top of the house, this had a pointed ceiling and the daylight came through a skylight in the sloping roof. To pay for violin lessons and other extras, Mother took in washing which she did in the cellar under the house, and Alice ran errands for the neighbours for pennies and half pennies.

Shopping was much easier in town. Every street seemed to have a shop at the corner which sold everything from firewood to cough medicine, sweets to needles and cotton, bread to vegetables. If the shop had an "off licence", this meant the proprietor could sell beer, stout, wines and spirits to be consumed off the premises. Tradesmen came round with their goods on carts; delivery boys on bicycles would bring orders from the larger shops in town; and all seemed hustle and bustle after the tranquillity of the country. The children's sleep was frequently disturbed by the noisy homecoming of merry makers from the many public houses, or the shouts of the "knockers up", and then the early clatter of boots and clogs on the pavement as factory and mill workers began their long day. Alice could not help but contrast the grimy pallid faces of the home-going workers with the ruddy outdoor complexions of the country-bred family. She felt an aching sympathy for the sooty-faced colliers. How terrible to work under the ground out of sight of the sun and sky.

Instead of the crystal-clear streams and dykes of the rural fens, the dark flowing river and manmade canals were near the family's new home. Barges were passing along the canal every day, carrying coal or grain to the coal yards or maltsters. On the river banks were four or five storeyed malting buildings where barley was spread on the floor to sprout ready for use in beer making. The aroma from the openings in the malt kilns was nearly as nice as that in the kitchen on baking day. Although the slatted shutters were closed at night, you could still see and hear, through the slits, the rats and mice scampering there. Not the sleek water rats and timid field mice of the farmlands, but horrid mangy looking rats and dirty house mice. When he saw them George would clench his fists and long for his ferrets to set them onto the vermin.

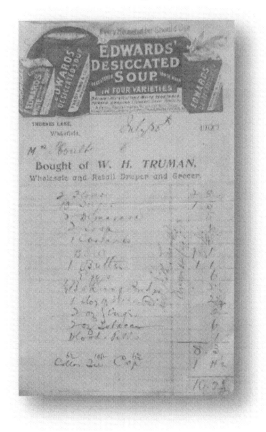

More money had to be spent on food as there were none of the farmyard inhabitants to use. Father was able to rent a piece of land nearby where he planted vegetables and built a makeshift hen run. All the household scraps were boiled up and mixed with meal to make a mash for the hens. George was not allowed to have ferrets, but with Father's help, had begun to keep a few pigeons.

Shopping in town

Saturday was one of the main shopping times. At the market in town, the stallholders would reduce their prices in order to sell the residue of their produce. For only a few pence Mother could buy a rabbit plus turnips, potatoes, carrots and onions for a stew. Fish was very cheap and Mother could make a delicious dish from cods' heads or skate knobs. Alice loved to accompany Mother into the market. The big naphtha lamps hanging over the stalls hissed and flared as Mother went from stall to stall seeking the best bargains.

The toffee pullers were a show in themselves. In spotless white overalls, they boiled the ingredients on portable stoves, then turned the sticky mess out onto oiled marble slabs. This toffee was rolled and kneaded into a pliable sausage shape, then thrown over a large metal hook hanging at the side of the stall. Next, one of the stallholders pulled the sweet sausage out until it was twice its original length, then looped it again over the hook. Pull and loop, pull and loop, in a smooth rhythm till the strand of toffee had reached the correct consistency and thickness. The toffee was then laid back on the slab and cut into bite-sized pieces with large metal shears.

The mixture of smells from the market was very appetising, and sometimes Mother would buy a "penny dip" for her willing basket carrier. This was a bread cake cut in half, dipped into hot pork dripping, sprinkled with salt and finished with a slice of fried onion. It tasted all the better when eaten in the open air as they toured the market.

As children easily do, Alice and her siblings soon adapted themselves to life in town. The strangeness felt when they used to come on holiday became, for a while, a reality. But neither Father nor Mother were happy away from the land and, although wages were lower, they felt the quality of life in the country was worth returning to. It was with great joy that the children heard they were to move back to farm life. Some things would be missed, but oh the pleasure to be able to breathe really fresh air again! Not the horrible smelly, soot-laden atmosphere of the town with its ghastly choking winter fogs and dirty streets. To be able to smell the new-mown hay, wild honeysuckle, the warm sweet breath of the cows, was worth so much. Once more the family uprooted themselves and moved back into the environment they loved: the world of broad horizons, growing crops and nature at her best.

The End

Alice

ABOUT THE AUTHOR

Elizabeth Laughton Corney was born in Yorkshire in 1926. She now lives in France, having moved there in 2006. Her mother Alice was born into a farm worker's family and grew up in Lincolnshire at the end of the 19th century and very early 20th century. Elizabeth heard many true stories of Alice's childhood in rural Lincolnshire, and has set them down to provide an informative and entertaining insight to life at that time.

Printed in Great Britain
by Amazon